Ouroboros

New Women's Voices Series, No. 183

poems by

Lissa Batista

Finishing Line Press
Georgetown, Kentucky

Ouroboros

New Women's Voices Series, No. 183

ACKNOWLEDGMENTS

I'd like to thank the following places for publishing the following poems:

Azahares Literary Magazine—"My Grandmother's Farmhouse"
Chautauqua—"North Bay Village Ghazal"
Drunk Monkeys—"Sex Manual"
New Note Poetry—"Sleeping Venus"
New York Quarterly—"The Milk Lady"
Tint Journal—"Daily Horoscope for My Mother", "Portrait of my Mother
Defanging a Snake at 13", "Leo Ego"
West Trade Review—"Dreaming in Brazil"

Publisher: Leah Huete de Maines
Editor: Christen Kincaid
Cover Art: Christina Gonzalez
Author Photo: Lissa Batista
Cover Design: Elizabeth Maines McCleavy

Order online: www.finishinglinepress.com
also available on amazon.com

Author inquiries and mail orders:
Finishing Line Press
PO Box 1626
Georgetown, Kentucky 40324
USA

Contents

To my mother and the women in my family

Dreaming in Brazil
after Eliot Weinberger

In Brazil, during springtime, we wake up in samba clothes. We wear pink goat's beard tucked in metal caged bras, goose feathers for the head piece. Beads fringe the lining of our underwear, our hips bouncing to the beat of brewing coffee on the stove.

In Brazil, the cops are robbers. The robbers are rich. The rich are natives in the amazon forests, dancing for rain. The rain, a guide to God.

In Brazil, the morning coffee makes itself.

There was a padaria on the corner from grandma's house, *Babaloos* of every color next to boxes of *Prestigio* chocolates under the counter where they sold Sonhos, donuts cut in half and filled with *Doce de Leite*. I'd have enough coins to buy a *Pitchula* soda, and wait outside for the *churrasqueiro* to grill skewered, chicken hearts in the afternoon. I ate chicken hearts like green grapes—popping one by one, squirting its juice on the sidewalk through my gapped-tooth smile.

When I eat chicken hearts, I think I'm the Evil Queen eating my heart out.

In Brazil, we kill backyard dogs with rat poison tucked inside a raw beef meatball. We roll it under iron gates or toss it over the 8-foot brick wall our grandfathers built.

In Brazil, everyone owns two-guns minimum. To have the right to own a gun, we kill one family member.

In Brazil, to dream of a coiled snake means someone is gossiping about you.

I dreamt of my hands covered with coils of baby snakes as I watched a burning helicopter crash into a bay, the snakes falling from my hands into the water. The next morning, my cousin shot and killed a man for spreading rumors about them cheating on their wife.

In Brazil, the sun is a red ball.

My great-grandmother poisoned her husband with rat killing chemicals in his *galinhada* at lunch time. My aunt, a teenager, dropped her infant sister from a hammock on the porch. My cousin shot a man they thought was their father.

In Brazil, my mother was a Beauty Pageant Queen. To get there, she had to kill a cow—make a hatchet, use the blunt side, strike the cow between the eyes. The cow kneels down, then lies on its side.

Go to Bahia's Carnaval if you love concerts. The locals gather white or in costumes, everything is a joke to mock the rich. Go to Rio's Carnaval to witness the culture of giant floats the size of small buildings, of choreographed dancing, of the samba that wears on anyone's feet: from the stiletto Pradas to Havaianas to feet bared in red mud, feet rainbows on CopaCabana.

In Brazil, women get away with murder.

Slit the neck, like knifing peanut butter out of the jar, drain the blood for twenty minutes. On the side facing us, skin her while she still bleeds the Brazilian Flag.

My cousin never gets caught. After 48-hours, the police stop the pursuit.

To dance samba, the women wobble their hips on the balls of their feet. They tiptoe in half moon patterns; step up then bring it back with a wave. Repeat on the other side. The two half moons, a rainbow.

The men dance samba on the balls of their feet.

After my mother killed the cow, she had to battle her father in the front yard, everyone watching. She was not allowed weapons, but she cheated and kept a knife in her back pocket.

In Brazil, we are the villain and the victim.

Hang the cow. Remove the skin from the other side with the sharpest knife you have. Remove the legs by cutting into the knee joints. Chop off the head. Save the hooves. Make *Mocoto*.

In Brazil, the slaves won independency with a meia-lua kick to the colonizer's face. That's why Capoeira is Brazil's favorite song.

In Brazil, we pray to the half moon.

In Brazil, the cow head is put to dry, to become the scarecrow on the cornfields, sugarcane fields, coffee fields, sunflower fields, empty fields, because Brazilians buy land but can't grow.

When I knew my parents weren't going to last, we were passing car-sized termite hills on the side of the roads. Ten years before this moment, I tried to knock them down. I kicked at it, mounds as tall as my 8 year-old body, made of clay. I imagined inside a complicated maze with cozy, cramped homes. Giant mounds, but they were in it together. I wondered how long I could keep my parents together in the shell of our car passing sunflower fields and termite hills.

Open the stomach, remove the organs—the heart, the stomach, liver, kidneys. In Brazil, we eat those, too. From tail to neck, separate the body with a knife, half and half, left rib and right rib. A butterfly.

In Brazil, we will eat everything.

Go to Carnaval in any other city and the locals have their TV on Globo, watching samba schools from a distance. Go to their open windows, they will give you wine in plastic cups, a plate of galinhada. The people at the bar will eat with you. The late night grandmothers will walk you home. You wake up to coffee brewing, rainbows of people outside your door. More food. More wine.

In Brazil, the stars are bigger than the moon. The night sky is the movie theater.

My aunt ground glass with pestle and mortar, the same way Brazilians do with garlic and salt, for seasoning. She sprinkled the glass like sugar over the rice pudding, his favorite. She added cinnamon powder over it to stop the glass from glistening. He took a bite. He knew. He ate the whole bowl.

In Brazil, we don't drive at night. Once, my father hit a horse when I was a baby in the front seat with my mother.

In Brazil, when the cow is being killed, they kneel to pray to god for our forgiveness.

My mother says she dreamt of horses the day she stabbed her father in the eye.

The year my parents separated, my dad went to Carnaval for the last time. While he was there, I slept in the bed with my mother and we both dreamt that we were under water, dredging slowly through the sand, the water so clear we could see an octopus walking, snakes sleeping in coils. Ink comes from above and blankets us like a thick carpet. An unbreathable darkness.

Carnaval is recording the samba school parade from Rio, and only watching your favorites. Carnaval is making pão de queijo, adding an extra tablespoon of cane sugar to your coffee. Carnaval is a house party that samba out into the neighboring streets. Carnaval é pagode, axé, forró, sertanejo, batucadas. Carnaval is family. Carnaval are pamonhas wrapped in corn husks. Carnaval is wearing white, or bikinis sequined in goat's beard, peacock-feathered headdresses. Carnaval is home.

In Brazil, when we die, we go to Carnaval.

Ode to Our 15-year American Anniversary

The kettle whistles with the morning birds on the bougainvilleas
outside our kitchen window. Over the stove, it spouts a hot bath

into our twenty-year-old immigrant carafe; white, peeling plastic,
printed with orange and red Brazilian wild-flowers, a parting gift—

my mother brews her Bustelo coffee, the blooming clumps
like barnacles under the wooden dock in the backyard.

Leo Ego

My narcissism are silver Victorian mirrors,
two precisely placed to the left and right
from the golden lacquered claw foot tub—
so when I wear bubbles like a pompadour
with froth pearls around my frank-and-myrrh
massage oiled neck, I can masturbate
by myself. Meditatively. Full eye contact.

Daily Horoscope for My Mother
February 15, 1974; Aquarius

Those born on this date display ingenuity as well as imagination, like when you took my brother and me to the backyard and told us ants were our friends. Our hands, triangle shaped, trapping little black ants until they crawled on us. The game was who could let the ant get the farthest up their arm. Me and Andy played for hours, ants dimpling up our shoulders black, like walking moles, as we outstretched our hands to the floor. Our fingers, their lift gates.

They often choose the path less traveled; there was a beautiful bartender who kept flashing her tits at father the first year the nightclub opened. You came to work through the back door, found her in the bathroom stall. You grabbed the girl's shoulders, slammed her to the wall. You opened your legs to hip width and brought your arm to the girl's throat, shoulders balled. You lifted her up from the floor about 6 inches. She was choking and scratching at your arm and face, you didn't budge.

They tend to live largely in their own head. When snakes feel attacked, they stand their ground. It took the security guard, the manager, and my father to rip you off from the girl. Her body, going limp. You recoiled. My father was yelling, telling you to go back to the house. To never come back. You left the way you came in. On the drive, you imagined ants finding homes in our elbow pits in the backyard. The nightclub in the rearview, a hill of neon lights.

A Love Letter

Tonight, I'm opening my door to strangers, your favorite thing. I don't mean to start off sarcastically, but I'm eating the licorice you've peeled apart from the Halloween assorted candy bags from previous years—the taste of licorice reminding me of October mornings, when hungover clouds drag past the sun like blankets, my face in your armpit bouquet, the smell of licorice and corn.

Outside is an autumn yellow, the same color of your aura, or so I told you once. Yellow light frequents around you in dominant amounts, your skin, a Tuscan sun; set me on fire. Your eyes like canaries, stalk me down by the sunflower fields. More memories of yellow.

I miss the way dimples dotted your cheek when you held laughs in arguments.

As my footprints turned into spumes that got carried away by soft waves, I thought of the times we went to the beach together. We would sit in the night under an audience of stars, watching the platform of waves tumble seashells on the sand mass, crowd surfing. We spoke about the night we had met, the things in between, how the future could've been if I met you a few months earlier, or a few years from now.

I miss your voice, the way you say *peeks* instead of *pizza*.

I've been thinking a lot about you lately. I think of you when It's 7 in the morning, the grass molding into morning fog as I drink my coffee in your mug. I think of you in the fall, when leaves quit on trees, leaving skeletons behind, a corporation of bone branches in front yards.

Before us, I would have never hemmed past city skies. For a while, we were Jack Nicholson and Morgan Freeman: best friends, worldly travelers, kicking fucks into the air, kicking things off our bucket list—

smoke weed in Kingston,
eat shawarmas in Jerusalem,
play house off the coast of Ibiza,
have sex in a tent at Walmart.

The sunflowers are smaller this year, they bow to the twilight, wilting, waiting for tomorrow's sun. Their bright smiley faces decay into heavy heads like dried out pancakes, brown scarecrows. I hope we'll see each other soon, but this time with canaries in your eyes, setting me on fire, of fucks we don't give but fucks we could have. Your Tuscan-sun skin smoldering gold during the summer, and I, your Icarus. I wish it was natural, us friends again, sharing conversations like bars of soap in our bathroom, no snarks, just ass grabs and craft beers—us like sunflowers, tracking the Sun's movement until dusk, our heads on the same bed we once called home.

On second thought, I hate licorice, too.

VHS Tape of my Parent's Wedding

My parents marry in Grandma's farmhouse,
in the middle of December's summer,
in Brazil, where girls made their own dresses—
my maternal grandma wore bright fuchsia
like the wedding flowers in mother's limp hands,
mother's mouth cupping the color scowl-red,
my father's sweat-rings through his twill jacket.
After I Dos, his sister cuts his tie to sell
to guests—money for their honeymoon.
During their first dance, they make out with tongue,
and I cry every time I watch this part;
It's her hands forever-holding his neck,
his arms around her waist, a tear gliding
down his shaven cheek, wetting their latched mouths.

My Mother Sees the Future

An old woman in white with logs in her hands
visited Mother as the moon snagged on the hills.
Her face, finger-smudged, her feet, a drag

underneath her, the tops of her toes peeled pink.
The kitchen door opened, a fruit bat fluttered in.
The old woman in white with logs in her hands

stopped at the foot of Mother's bed. Mother had known
ghosts since her newborn bottom lip split; an accident.
The old woman's face, finger-smudged, dragged her feet

to another room where her brothers slept,
deep into their third dreams as Mother followed.
The old woman in white with logs in her hands

told eight-year-old Mother she had come to retrieve
another—Mother prayed to be taken instead.
The old woman, finger-smudged to her feet

drops a waterfall of logs outside the kitchen door.
On her brother's shirt found on the lawn, fruit bat wings
stuck to its collar—an omen. The old woman's
finger smudged feet still drag through Mother's dreams.

A Soap Opera of Us

It's you; towering in tight slacks, hair in a ponytail, a curl caresses
your forehead, we know how much you need to be touched.

It's you; looking through my phone, checking my purse
for clues about the person. I watch in a red dress, drinking red—

whining about your coworker, the one who lives in Canada,
who texted you about a song that reminded her of you. You're mad

because I'm mad. The camera close-ups on my tears—my face
villainous-fat, eyebrows furrowed, hair frizzed and lips overlined.

Red is the blood in my ears when I find you and her in the lobby,
red is the handprint on your face. Red are the claws

down her back, the cop car lights outside, my flushed cheeks
in an overnight jail, red is the fire in my underwear when the cop

on duty was my high school boyfriend who hadn't changed—
the uniform strangles his biceps, his radio cinches to his chest,

the wire brushes his nipple. Red is his mouth when we kiss,
red is my ass. He smacks so hard, another cop calls backup.

He presses me against the wall, his body flush on my back,
legs wide, he dares me to move. I feel him through his pants—

I lift my cheek from against the wall and lick his lips, a growl
zippers between his teeth, but before I fuck to forget about you,

you bail me out. No ponytail. Wrinkled shirt. Time to go home.
It's you: a cigarette sitting on a smirk, windows down, wild hair,
    hand on my thigh.

Sex Manual

Anything goes—anal, a backdoor man, beads of sweat, glossy
beads, glass beads, plastic beads, ben wa balls, balls deep, a rosary
cross to cut cocaine chased with cocktails on the bar, you
dirty dog, give me some sugar, daddy, dirty martinis for the ladies
eagerly drawn faces, egging each other on, in stalls, an experiment,
fairy queens fingering each other's thoughts and glory holes, who
grew up on Game Boys and cable; channel 99—girls on girls gone
hot-and-ready, getting horny, baby? Hand-solo that hard on.
I am a wet dream, I am the WAP, I am the warning, I am a Sex-Jedi,
jukeboxing your mind, I'm Doja Cat, random erections for extra
kicks, IYKYK, a kosher knob slobbing, corn on the cob, gawk 3000.
Listen and look, lickety split my labia like licorice, your sticky lips,
masturbate in front of me, own the masc, mouth off on my pussy,
naughty girls, nuzzle the fuzz on my face, all nymphos welcome,
orgasmic aphrodisiac octopi squirt too, give me ocean pink, stop
pussy-footing around. Plug it in, pile driver, pickle-me-tickle-me,
Queen of Queers, let's queef shamelessly, let's quickie in stalls, let's
roughhouse, raw dog, then rusty trombone, around-the-clock.
Spit or swallow? Spread eagle or spoon fuck? Spit it out already.
Tail flowers don't deter me, let's trib 'til tap out while teabagging.
Undress me, undo me, unload up the dirt road. I'm hyper-
ventilating. On the verge. In the valley of love lies Venus, face first.
Well-hung wanker, whalebone the wind tunnel, wiggling toes.
X-mas came early, so did you. I'm Santa Clause, bitch—so giving.
Yodel into my yellow canal while I yank your yo-yo. You're done.
Zip it good, zipper up, zoom out, clear history, open new tab.

Portrait of My Mother Defanging a Snake at 13

Her dirty blonde hair camouflages her long, lanky body. She's in a t-shirt and underwear, tarantulating through the forest in her backyard on all fours.

She puts her ear to the ground, the buzz of the earth coming alive. Her body rises like corn stalk, her hair over her shoulders like haystack, her eyes needling through the mound of dead leaves a yard in front of her.

Her mouth waters as she watches the jararaca's scales expand; the snake tastes no fear in the air. My mother has fooled him, but she is no prey. She inhales through her nose as the snake straightens. Its back rattling out from the coils. The snake slithers four feet to her left and it's too late.

In a swift move, my mother's limbs web through the cool dirt, pinching the snake head between her left thumb and pointer finger, her right hand on its tail. My mother meditates; she gardens.

The jararaca: its face a root being pulled from the ground towards her. She lets go of its tail. Her right hand cradles its head, her left fingers patiently extracts a fang like a child's milk tooth.

One, then the other.

A Lineage of Things

Things my mother learns before becoming a mother: defang a snake, hold a knife, shoulder a shotgun, fight a man, talk back to ghosts, ride a bull, tip a cow, milk a cow, inseminate a cow, cut the balls off a bull and sell it to the market, sew a dress, cook rice and beans, hold a cigarette but never smoke it.

The night my parents meet in Brazil, my dad is waiting at her table where she sits with her father and her best friend. My father drapes his American-bought leather jacket over her, she follows him to the bathroom and comes back to the table with his gum in her mouth.

Things my father learns before becoming a father: sell popsicles, shine shoes, dive off bridges, how to treat syphilis, open a church, open a pharmacy, open dime bags, cross the border, live in Boston, open a restaurant, don't hide the joint, smoke it.

I asked my mother what did she learn before becoming a mother after I make this list, she texts me back and misspells cows, "help my father put a baby caw inside the caw. Cut off the balls from the male caws."

My mother had me in her arms when they crashed the car, my dad hit a horse. The horse buckled up the roof of the car and smashed the window in. It was supposed to be romantic—driving with no headlights on to see the Milky Way, but my mother is afraid of the dark. She agrees only to stay with him if he takes her to America.

I still have specks of scars from the glass on my face from the night of the accident.

My parents in America kissed over plates of steaks at Las Vacas Gordas. They danced anywhere music played, my dad holding a firm grip on my mother's ass. In every picture my mother holds a hand, jeweled with a new ring over my dad's chest, the places change: Jamaica, Mexico, Brazil, New York, Turkey, Greece, the beach, Mango's, Santa's Enchanted Forest.

When my parents signed the divorce papers, they didn't have a Nicole Kidman moment.

Things I learn before becoming a mother: how to cheat at pin the tail on the donkey, sell candy out of my bookbag in middle school, hit back, cook rice, dive in the water so it doesn't make a noise, bartend, smoke a cigarette with a joint on the other hand.

"I didn't learn much."

Graveyard Shifts

A few months after our first breakup,
 the taste of your name is a bucket filled to the brim
of out-of-season blackberries, leaving behind
a rot, to help forget what your lips felt like,

that your hair smelled of jasmines at night
when we smoked cigarettes in my backyard.
You called me sugar once, or twice, when you slept
over. You were proud of our makeshift fort

made with a podium of pillows. You called me
sugar under white blanket waves,
we were embroidered doilies; arms out,
a dangle of legs, hands never touching.

I won't tell you about my frequent trips
to graveyard shift diners
and how they sit me at tables for two
because pretty ladies don't eat alone.

Under the moon's faint glow awaiting
the breakfast crowd, I sit on the diner's curb
to fumble with a cigarette under puppet shadows
of stringy branches and rogue leaves.

I fingerpaint the asphalt in oils from cars
that came before us. I paint blackberries,
your dirty hair. I paint until the ashes of my cigarette
drag my attention to dawn's neon skies.

I paint your rippling pool eyes,
a kaleidoscope of forget-me-nots.
Then I smear the picture
with the palm of my hand.

Seven in the morning; my neighbors
are waking up, their kids in maple smiles

from pancakes, the mailman a little too early,
the morning sun bathing on clay roofs.

I can see it now, you slouched over
your swinging feet, shirtless and a little sweaty
from dreams you've always kept to yourself.
A syrup of curls across your forehead.

The Milk Lady

i.

What an honor to be called the name my ancestors gardened
on callused hands, the name of a labored body, the name of women
without husbands—as if it is a bad thing to have more lovers than

divorces—name of morning, name of strong arms pumping shots
from a cow's thick-skinned udder into a tin bucket, a skill set,
the name of sexy vintage pinup ads, the way you meant it—a slut.

ii.
I tattoo a portrait
of a spotted cow,
you come closer
and grip my arm,
laugh at your own
joke, *what are you
the milk lady?*
and I, with big tits,
my camel toe
eating
my leggings,
flirting with anyone,
my kindness
is *fucking slutty.*

iii.
The Milk Lady is a No Man's Land; is a long walk on the beach
during the afternoon sun in Miami with no shoes on; is a callused,
no nail-polish, hand; is long-colored hair eddying in the wind with
split ends; is a small cavity; is a type everyone wants to know but
not befriend; is a Libra moon; is to have been loved many times in
every country; is mediterranean blue; is a crystal quartz bathtub
with running cold water in October; is a tired brow; is a thirty
year old mother who spends her days teaching language arts to
kids who'd rather be on Snapchat; is playing Nintendo Switch with

her son; is forgetting to cook dinner; is forgetting that mother also means sexy; is fatherly advice, *everything: people, milk, love, expires;* is insomnia; is a bite of mango with the browning peel; is anyone; is me

North Bay Village Ghazal

Mother with a bowl of thawed shrimp,
    a sand bucket, and two fishing rods.
She dresses the hook in bait,
    shoots the line from the first rod.

Her body curves out, reels in, the line's
    over the horizon—a contrail in the sky.
I see her exhale, the bobber in the water;
    a shrimp hits rock bottom, corroding.

Me and Andy race on the deck;
    I slide like an 80s song in socks.
My mother catches a lobster;
    a lionfish nibbles, teases, leaves the rod.

Our sand bucket stays empty,
    mother reels in the venomous ones.
I flick the hook through
    Andy's belly button with the second rod.

Andy's belly button, a fish mouth;
    he brags he's Christina Aguilera.
Mother's hair, a flag wavering;
    tugging the line in a lullaby, she loosely rods.

Mother relaxes, her thoughts in waves,
    her eyes shore far away from here.
The bay lights flicker on,
    my feet hurt, mother reels in the rods.

I can't walk. I sit on a plastic pool chair
    as mother slides off my socks.
Li, your feet filled with splinters; my mother holds
    Andy over her shoulder, I hold the rods.

In another life, Mother would hold me in her left arm,
    my brother cradled in her right.
The bucket of poisonous fish would be dumped,
    a push with her foot; left on the deck, the rods.

My Grandmother's Farmhouse

I remember the smell of earth that incensed once the rain came, the red dirt ran bloody and dried a heavy brown. Whatever shoe or shirt stayed outside would have to be thrown away because the dusting of the red dirt hardened on the clothesline or in the creases of sneakers.

I remember the chipped paint on the outside walls that did its best to cover the thick cement and clay bricks.

Chicken coops, man-made lakes, cemetery owls perched on the branches of the anga tree, small monkeys swinging, snakes in the shrubs.

Every celebration was baptized with an animal from the farmhouse. We used mostly chickens. Grandmother would go into the coop and snap the neck. *Hold the neck as if you were holding a rope. Pull, then twist.*

Take the dead chicken. Swing it around and above your head. Let it go. Make sure it slams onto the wall. We repeated until bored or until my aunt finished cutting the watermelon from the vines in the garden.

My uncle wore jeans, a silver belt buckle with a skull of a cow imprinted on it. His leather boots, crimson-creased with clay. A straw hat. A dark button down, rolled sleeves. A pocket knife, 6 inches, on the hook of his waist.

A black pig was wagoned onto a concrete slab that covered the water well. I extended an arm out. My fingertips smoothing its thick, warm skin, reminding me of my mother brushing my hair from my face as I cried hot tears. The pig opened up his eyes, he let out one more squeal and kicked off the slab. My uncle was faster: slit its neck.

My uncle took a flamethrower to the pig, burned off the bristled hairs, the skin. The smell of burnt body lingers in this memory. An incision around every limb, an incision from neck to anus, incisions to remove all organs, burying only the intestines.

In the beginning of this memory, a black pig escaped from the pig pen and made its way to the skirts of the forest. He was free: he wasn't fast. My uncle enters the frame. His knife held up towards the sky, a sun in his hand. Then, one arm was around the pig's neck, the other under his flank. Pan out to the cemetery owls, the chicken coop, small monkeys swinging over red dirt. I imagine it was a hug. The knife in his neck, a carry-on bag. My uncle was saying goodbye. The black pig, free.

Letters to the Celtic Cross Tarot Spread During Full Moon in Scorpio

1.   Heart of the Matter
The Queen of Pentacles relaxes her robe, shoulders glittering with sweat after pulling the weeds that grow too close to her hedges. A mother figure. She enjoys all things worldly—cooking and creating. I envy the feeling of making broccoli and chicken: stereo on blast, some crooner crying about love or sadness, my hands working the wooden spoon. Instead, I throw away a third bag of soggy spinach from the veggie cupboard in the fridge.

2.   Challenge
The Fool lives on the edge of a new adventure. I know he's acting out my most intrusive thoughts: leaving my lover at the house of the married blonde woman with the flat stomach; cheeks so chubby, he doesn't remember her eye color. They spent nights in Vegas; where they spoke of the universe, of her marriage, of work—how fucking boring.

3.   Unconscious
A fence of nine wands I'm leaning on. Horizon thick with anchored clouds as I recall what I've done to win him back: follow him to the bar, park my car outside his house, call 104 times in a row. Should I regret showing up at brunch with his friends, spinning the car, banging his window to see if I could break the glass? I've sobbed at red lights, I've sobbed at a kiddie park, I've sobbed in the paper aisle at Publix. Tonight, he will cook me dinner when I get home.

4.   Past
The Knight of Pentacles sits on his black horse, the pentacle in his hand, a crystal ball. In it, I see their day together; gold is her hair when she drops off his work laptop at our house; he kisses her. His mom watches from the window. But the knight sees nothing, nothing but me. His frown deepens, he scolds; *did hard work need to be done? that the work hasn't yielded all that you have hoped for? to keep him?*

5.   Conscious

Three swords point to a body in a coffin, where another sword is stored. Like my heart in my throat when his phone vibrates.

6.   Future

A Page of Wands, a child, a new spark. Maybe this is the couple's therapy session I keep asking for instead of another fight about whose turn it is to feed the dog. Maybe it's the birthday gift he didn't give me last month. Maybe it's the weekend getaway in Vegas. Maybe it's a spa day at The Standard. I wonder if her husband knows.

7.   Querent

Ten of Cups is a family circle. Motherhood; the wave that crashed into my home and hermit body. What if I couldn't hold it all together? My son sits on the shore, I forgot the blanket. My shoulders, pink from sunburn. No ice in the cooler. Gnats I can't see biting at our feet. We came to watch the waves—today, the water is still. Another family builds a castle on the beach. *But it's sand*, I say.

8.   Environment

A bedroom decorated with Nine Swords. To the lady under the covers, this must be frightening. I, too, often see things in the dark. Her blonde hair, my stretch marks, the space between us in the queen-sized bed. Years ago, I wished for this space. I hated how our thighs insulated sweat that dripped down the backs of my knees. Now I long to feel the backs of his knees again.

9.   Hopes and Fears

The Queen of Wands is ablaze. She tears pages of my insecurities, sets them on fire. Your small ass? *rip*. Your separation? *rip*. Your sobs? *rip*. Your sandcastle? *rip*. Your fucks? *rip*. When she's done, I'm all spine. I'm taller than Liberty. I use the clouds like anchors and blow them into balloons. I take the crown..

10. Outcome

Isn't the purpose of life free will? The Seven Cups are opportunities, a snake, a jewel, a red-and-white bouquet, a dragon, a wreath of victory, a blanket, a bucking tower. The Fool never looks down when grazing the lips of sand-gold mountains. He doesn't choose a cup. Me? I hesitate. I leap.

Self Portrait as Juliet

I'm from the land where women tame
snakes in the garden, taking the body
like Eucharist: swallow whole: burp the alphabet:
leave crumbs around the lips: a reward.
Tell me I can't, and I'll defy in red, I'll anal,
I'll spit thicker than Rose in Titanic,
then I'll suck it back up; I'll hawk.
Show me a man; if he winks first, we're fucking.
If he stays over, meet me at the altar with Elvis,
his suit boutonnièred with fake flowers, hiding angina.
This is not a suicide note,   but I'm tired
of listening to my heart: I stand on the balcony,
I hear my favorite song, I follow a glimpse of him
through salt water aquarium, overdose on his love.
See? It's never worth the heartbreak.

Exit Interview: A Google Search of When to Leave Your Partner
After Roger Reeves

How do they make you feel about yourself?

The last time I was cheated on,
I begged you to tell me the colors
of her labias—if she flowered
over your fuzzed mustache
or clamped your flat tongue.
Did stems from her fingernails break
out, white and permanent,
over the garden of her hips?
When she touches up her roots,
whose hands shovel through
her plastic-dandelion hair?

My body is in winter.
My branch-brown strands
raked in slivers of snow,
Everything my body held up
has fallen inches from years before—
I imagine I am the evil queen
asking who is fairest of them all,
when she just wanted the love
of someone who would love her back.
Hag and all. Hag and all. Hag and all.

Do you feel free when you're together?

My son and I play a middle finger game.
He holds a bag and tells me to throw up
an imaginary ball. The ball falls heavy
into the bag—he pulls out his middle finger
pointing it sharply at me. We laugh so hard
it's easy to picture milk pouring from our noses.
In this memory, think of my son's almond eyes
when he saw me looking for something

in my pocket. Instead of candy, it's my middle finger
We flash middle fingers, eat sour gummies,
but we only play this way when Daddy isn't home.

What was the turning point?

In the tarot spread, the Devil covets the Three of Swords:
     The moon, drunk, spilling over the clouds—
     tries to find a way home.

The boundary between day and night is called terminator;
     In the movie, Arnold's mission is to kill the girl,
     his promise to always come back for her.

I prayed for a man who lives forever, relentless, whose only mission
     is to go back in time and have me. Only me. The Terminator,
     like the boundary, predictable. He always comes back to me.

The moon sobers up after an all-nighter:
     ghosts or frosted glass or onions sauteed in a pan.
     Now the sun faces the moon. They breakfast in the sky. No
     boundaries.

If you're the moon, I want to be nocturnal:
     but in this poem, the moonbeams don't come home
     until morning, and I'm too tired to open up the door.

Tarot tells a journey. I hope for a different ending.
     What if we could go back in time?
     What if we did—and you still left?

*Have you thought of how life could be if you ended things with your
partner?*

I have pancakes for dinner, my night light is on,
the dog is on the bed with the cat, who sleeps
in the covers. I come home and I kick a left shoe
in the kitchen, the other at the curtains because I can
make as much fucking noise as I want. I fart. I fart so much.

I download then uninstall Tinder after ten matches,
just for the compliments. Tell me how beautiful I am.
But I come home alone,   always alone.
        My bed,   a solar system.
Atmospheric cold.
A skydive.
I sleep.

With Thanks

Thank you to my mother, who inspired most of my poems in this collection. Thank you to my brother for being my backbone. To dad for always believing in me to pursue whatever I wanted, the world is mine. To Brittany for giving this chapbook a lookover to make sure it was ready for the world's eyes. To Jaden for reading my entire manuscript and highlighting the poems that were working, which made it easy to birth this chapbook. To my guides, mentors, professors, and friends: Denise Duhamel, Julie Marie Wade, Campbell McGrath, and Les Standiford; for encouraging every sentiment, emotion, and word. Another shout out to Denise for pouring over every single poem with me, hyping me up to be even sexier, and sending me home with homework on erotic poetry, and to Julie Wade who implanted the seed of this chapbook, giving it a name and guiding me to follow the matriarchal string. I am so lucky. My gratitude extends to every colleague and friend I made at every workshop or conference I attended that gave meaningful, critical, and insightful care towards my poetry: Trey, Rani, and Rosa especially. I'll forever be grateful.

Thank you to my soulmate, Miles, for giving me everything I needed to give this a go. For reading every word without judgment, for influencing the authentic and loving places my mind wanders when diving into my work. I love you.

Lissa Batista is a Brazilian born poet living in Miami, Florida among iguanas and summer hurricanes. Batista earned a Bachelor's Degree in English from Florida International University in 2016 and an M.F.A. in Creative Writing, 2023. She has published poems and essays in *Prairie Schooner, New York Quarterly, Passengers Journal, Drunk Monkeys, Islandia, West Trade Review, South Florida Poetry Journal, Bellingham Review* and a few others. Batista was nominated for both Best New Poets and the Pushcart Prize, and a semi-finalist in the 2023 New Women's Voiced Chapbook Competition for Finishing Line Press.

www.ingramcontent.com/pod-product-compliance
Lightning Source LLC
Chambersburg PA
CBHW022044080426
42734CB00009B/1234